Study Pack for CELTA and Cert TESOL Students

Exercises in Grammar and Pronunciation used in EFL, ESOL and ESL Contexts

By

Pamela Benson

INTRODUCTION — How to use this Pack

Aims

This study pack is aimed at prospective and new ESOL/EFL teachers who will have to teach English grammar within lessons. For most, grammar is the most difficult part of teaching, so this book is intended as a reference guide and for practice purposes.

This pack focuses on three "core" CELTA areas: pedagogic grammar, teaching pronunciation, and English in its social and historical context.

The core reference text is **Practical English Usage** by Michael Swan, Oxford University Press, **ISBN: 9780194420983**. This text is standard for CELTA courses.

(The other reference texts, although not necessary for the completion of the study pack, have been chosen for their direct relevance to the ESOL/EFL/EAL teacher. *The Good Grammar Book* by Catherine Walter and Michael Swan, Murphy's *English Grammar in Use* and Kenworthy's *Teaching English Pronunciation* are invaluable reference books for the practising teacher. All give clear explanations of points, as well as guidelines for teaching. *Varieties of English*: *An Introduction to the Study of Language*, by Freeborn et al, puts the English, or Englishes we use today, into historic and social perspective. A careful reading of the first four chapters should help to answer many of the questions trainees often have about what 'correct' English is, and what is or isn't taught in the classroom).

How to use the Pack

Stage One—the texts

It's a good idea to buy all the above books for your own use, as they are the minimum that an ESOL/EFL/EAL teacher needs to know! The Walter and Swan and Murphy texts are a useful source of material in the classroom.

Stage Two—the pack

The pack is divided into three parts. The main body of work focuses on grammar and pronunciation. The *Grammar* section is highlighted in yellow, the *Pronunciation* in pink, *Varieties* in blue and the *Appendix* in green. The pack aims at a practical application of the points covered in the grammar book. Thus the Grammar section asks you to analyse language, giving pedagogic explanations and illustrations, as you would in the classroom. Some answer sheets ask you to quote a page reference to the grammar book. This is important, as you as a teacher must be able to use the texts readily as a source of information. It also requires you to be precise in your grammatical explanations, using the correct EFL/ESOL terminology. For this reason, you must avoid using the terms you have maybe used in the past, either at school or elsewhere, as often they are different from those used in the EFL/ESOL classroom.

Many of the worksheets in the *Grammar* section have incorrect sentences, which you are asked to analyse. All of these have been gleaned from actual students' work. The essay in answer sheet 7, for example, is reproduced verbatim from an essay written as homework. It is hoped that this will prepare you for the never-ending ESOL teacher's task of language analysis and subsequent explanation, and also give those of you with limited classroom experience a taste of students' work.

The first part of the pack is the section on **Grammar**. There are 7 study sheets and 7 answer sheets.

N.B. The terms 'progressive' (as in present progressive) and 'continuous' (as in present continuous) are synonymous/interchangeable. The present continuous/progressive of 'I swim' is 'I am swimming'.

The second part of the pack focuses on **Pronunciation**. This has a set of 4 answer sheets, with corresponding study sheets.

Part three uses the **Varieties** text, and contains just one answer sheet.

There is also a short **Appendix** to further explain any language points.

Good luck and enjoy yourself!

GRAMMAR – STUDY SHEET 1

Referring to Appendix, Study Sheet 1 and to Swan, Section 10 (see also index under 'tenses'), list on the Answer Sheet one or more of the following verb tenses and verb types found in the passage below. Please include the subjects with the verbs.

1. Present simple	8. Past simple passive
2. Present continuous	9. Infinitive
3. Future simple	10. Present participle
4. Present perfect active	11. Past participle
5. Present perfect passive	12. Modal verb
6. Past perfect	
7. Past simple active	

Island Paradise

"You are living" says Commander Briggs, "on an amazing island which contains everything you need to survive. You breathe its fresh air, you eat its natural food and you drink and wash in its clean water. While you are busy living your lives, the island provides for all your needs and is in contact with the outside world, following all news developments."

The island is so well inhabited that it is easy to forget that it is so isolated, being two thousand miles from land. Until recently, the commander had estimated that the island might only hold approximately eight hundred inhabitants. Now that that number has been reached, still new people arrive every minute of the day. In ten years there will be twice as many of them.

Initially the island had far fewer people; it had plenty of provision for future generations. The huts are well furnished. There are vast expanses of land, of forest and fields, where every kind of food can be grown. Rivers and oceans provide water and fish, and it was thought that below the land were buried countless precious resources, for special use in the future.

The commander is, however, worried. The islanders have begun to behave strangely. They don't seem to realise that the island has its limits. Many of the original supplies have been used up and resources have nearly been finished. Food and water isn't getting to the islanders equally. Some want to have first pickings, at the expense of others. Others are claiming monopolies on the land, or resources. Fighting on the island has caused the destruction of whole areas, and the death of many co-inhabitants.

But the biggest worry, and the most recent one, is that no one seems to realise that the remote island operates on a very delicate system. When the inhabitants arrived, the life-forms and eco-system were in balance, and the few inhabitants all got on with each other. Now the fighting is unbalancing the system for everybody. The quality of life on the island is deteriorating as the system breaks up.

Something must be done. It should have been done a long time ago. Commander Briggs is going to make an announcement. What will she say?

GRAMMAR – STUDY SHEET 2

Verb tenses: constituent parts
(See *Appendix*, Study Sheet 2)

Task
Label the tenses below, and, on the worksheet, select and mark the correct constituent part analysis for each verb tense. Note that a particular form may be applicable more than once.

Example
 1. He walks
Tense: present simple
Formed of: d

1. He finished	2. He has eaten
3. He has been working	4. He has been conned
5. He had escaped	6. He had been hoping
7. He had been conned	8. He will remember
9. He will be travelling	10. He will have been travelling
11. He will have been rescued	12. He might have been disappointed

a. auxiliary verb "have" in simple past form + auxiliary verb "be" in past participle form + present participle of main verb

b. auxiliary verb "have" in 3rd person singular form of present tense + auxiliary verb "be" in past participle form + present participle of main verb

c. modal verb + auxiliary verb "have" in base form + past participle of auxiliary verb "be" + past participle of main verb

d. base form of main verb + s

e. auxiliary verb "have" in 3rd person singular form of present tense + auxiliary verb "be" in past participle form + past participle of main verb

f. base form of main verb + ed

g. modal verb + auxiliary verb "be" in base form + present participle form of verb

h. modal verb + base form of main verb

modal verb + auxiliary verb "have" in base form + past participle of auxiliary verb "be" + present participle of main verb

i. modal verb + auxiliary verb "have" in base form + past participle of auxiliary verb "be" + present participle of main verb

j. auxiliary verb "have" in simple past form + auxiliary verb "be" in past participle form + past participle of main verb

k. auxiliary verb "have" in 3rd person singular form of present tense + past participle of main verb

l. auxiliary verb "have" in simple past form + participle of main verb

GRAMMAR – STUDY SHEET 3

A. Sentences 1-7 contain a wrong use of a verb tense.
B. Sentences 8-9 contain a wrong verb.
C. Sentence 10. Both sentences are grammatically correct, but each has a different meaning.

To guide you look at the list of verb forms on *Appendix, Study Sheet 1*, find the labels for the verb forms used (incorrect (b) and correct (c).

A Task 1-7
On the Study Sheet:
a. correct the error, i.e. rewrite the sentence
b. name the incorrect verb tense
c. name the correct verb tense
d. comment briefly on the use of the correct tense

Example: "I am here since 2010."
a. I have been here since 2010
b. present simple of verb to be
c. present perfect of verb to be
d. present perfect used with an action that started at an unspecified time in the past and which continues into the present. See *Appendix, Study Sheet 3*.

1." I will tell him about it when we will meet." (i.e. the telling will happen at a future date)	5. "I have lived in London for 2 years." (the speaker now lives in New York)
2. "I am smoking 20 cigarettes a day."	6. "She has had a bath, when the phone rang." (she was still in the bath when the phone rang)
3. "He has left his country 2 years ago."	7. "I smoked cigarettes ever since I can remember." (the speaker still smokes)
4. "She already ate breakfast when the post arrived."	

B Task: Write a brief paragraph discussing points 8 and 9 below.

8. A student asks why they <u>can't</u> abbreviate: "He's an athletic build" when they <u>can</u> abbreviate both: "He's got an athletic build", and "He's an athlete".
What's the reason? Can you think of other examples to illustrate this point?

9. A student who recently visited Windsor Castle writes "I'm really glad that we've been to Windsor Castle." Another student asks "Which verb is this? Shouldn't it be 'We've gone to Windsor Castle'?"
What do you reply?

C Task: Give an explanation of the meaning of each a and b, which focuses on the difference in meaning. c. Refer to *Appendix, Study Sheet 3*

10a. "I **used to** go camping"
10b. "I **am used to** camping"
10c. _____

GRAMMAR – STUDY SHEET 4

Regular and irregular verbs

Task:

Students learn irregular verbs (sometimes called "strong" verbs, but not usually by ESL teachers) by heart, and expect the teacher to instantly recite their three essential forms!

Write the simple past tense and past participle forms of the following verbs, and decide which verb type they fall into:

Type a, one form only;   type b, two forms;   or type c, three forms

If necessary, refer to a dictionary. If a verb has two possible forms for one tense, list both.

	Base form	simple past tense	past participle	type
Example	bite	bit	bitten	c
1.	cut			
2.	burn			
3.	become			
4.	outbid			
5.	lay			
6.	lie			
7.	arise			
8.	beat			
9.	be			
10.	dream			

Transitive and intransitive verbs

Task:

Refer to Appendix, Study Sheet 4 then identify the verbs underlined in the following sentences as either transitive: vt, or intransitive: vi. Don't forget that some verbs are either one or the other, while others can be used in both ways. Take the verb as used in the sentence. Be careful with passives, and with phrasal verbs.

Example:	Prices <u>dropped</u> in the summer	vi
	He <u>dropped</u> the plate	vt

1. He <u>eats</u> bananas but not kiwis _____
2. He does nothing but <u>eat</u> _____
3. She <u>rose</u> at dawn _____
4. The flag <u>was raised</u> at dawn _____
5. The boy <u>lay</u> down to sleep _____
6. He <u>laid</u> the book on the table _____
7. He <u>dropped</u> the eggs in Tesco _____
8. His face <u>dropped</u> at the mention of homework _____
9. She <u>ran</u> the length of the hall _____
10. She <u>ran</u> the risk of offending her boss _____

GRAMMAR – STUDY SHEET 5

Task 1. Conditionals (Refer to *Appendix, Study Sheet 5*)

Reorder the following sentences into three main conditional types. State the verb tenses used for the underlined verbs. The tenses are: past perfect, present form of would, present simple, future, past form of would, simple past.

If I <u>enjoyed</u> parachuting, I <u>would do</u> it again.
If I <u>enjoy</u> parachuting, <u>I will do</u> it again.
If I <u>had enjoyed</u> parachuting, I <u>would have done</u> it again.

1a   1st Type
        Tenses:

1b   2nd Type
        Tenses:

1c   3rd Type
        Tenses:

Many conditional sentences are based on a "suppose". The conditional sentence is contrary to fact. For example, "If I wanted, I could learn Somali", the fact is I don't want to learn Somali.

Look at the "fact" sentences below, and decide which of the conditional types listed above, they relate to.

                                                                                                                         Conditional type

1d. One refers to the future. I haven't been parachuting yet. It is a
possibility that I will enjoy it.   _____

1e. One refers to a past experience of parachuting and I hated it and
turned down the offer of doing it again.   _____

1f. One makes a general statement about my feelings about parachuting.
It is unclear whether I have been or not. To say I enjoy it would be
Untrue and it is doubtful I will do it again.   _____

Conditional sentences are generally taught as following certain tense sequences. See
1st, 2nd and 3rd Types. In fact however, conditional sentences can "mix" tenses, according to the fact, and the speaker's focus.

For example, a "regular" sequence might be:
Fact: You had an accident (simple past) because you didn't listen to me (simple past).
Conditional: If you had listened to me (past perfect) you would not have had an accident (past form of would). Type 3.

A "mixed" sequence might be:
Fact: You had an accident (simple past) because you never listen to me (simple present).
Conditional: If you listened to me (simple past), you wouldn't have had an accident (past form of would).
Mixed: Types 2 and 3.

CELTA Grammar & Pronunciation Study Pack by Pamela Benson ©2017

(Cont.) Task 2:

Now write the corresponding conditional sentences, and say which type of conditional you have used: types 1,2,3 or mixed, and give reasons (use 1d,e,f as a guide).

2. Fact: I ate the pizza and I felt sick.

Conditional: If_____

Type: _____

Reason: Fact: Both refer to a past experience.

3. Fact: I ate the pizza and I feel sick.

Conditional: If_____

Type: _____

Reason: _____

4. Fact: He smokes a lot and has difficulty breathing.

Conditional: _____

Type: _____

Reason: _____

5. Fact: The children are playing happily and she doesn't have a camera!

Conditional: _____

Type: _____

Reason: _____

6. Fact: He has an interview next week and he can't decide whether to go by train or coach.

Conditional: _____

Type: _____

Reason: _____

CELTA Grammar & Pronunciation Study Pack by Pamela Benson ©2017

GRAMMAR – STUDY SHEET 6

Articles

Task:

Refer to 'Rules of Use' below, Appendix, Study Sheet 6 *and Swan, Sections 62-69. Then read the sentences below, and on the worksheet, select and mark the "rule of use" which best explains the use, or emission of, the article. Note that the order of the "rules of use" has been mixed, and that a particular role may apply more than once.*

1. I always like to have a <u>drink</u> before going to bed.
2. The <u>radio</u> he gave me is a Sony.
3. <u>Vegetarians</u> don't eat meat.
4. <u>The car</u> has become a status symbol.
5. <u>Life</u> in developing countries can be hard.
6. <u>The life</u> I lead is full of surprises.
7. Blessed are <u>the poor</u>, for they shall inherit the earth.
8. Once there lived <u>an old man</u> in <u>a cottage</u>. <u>The old man</u> had <u>a daughter</u> called Jane.
9. Put the vase on <u>the TV</u>, it looks nice there.
10. I'm <u>an astronaut</u>, my husband's <u>a nurse</u>.
11. I'm going to <u>the post office</u>.
12. <u>The earth</u> is not as flat as we once thought, nor is <u>the moon</u> made of cheese!
13. She's at <u>school</u> today.
14. I'm going to a parents meeting at <u>the school</u>.

Rules of Use

a. We use "the" before singular countable nouns to denote something in particular.
b. We often use no article with uncountable nouns in general statements.
c. We use "a/an" with singular countable nouns, when the object is not specified.
d. We use "the" when it is clear to the listener which thing/place we mean.
e. We use "a/an" before jobs and professions.
f. We use an article when we refer to an institution in its non-functional sense.
g. We use no article with plural countable nouns to make general statements.
h. We use "a/an" when referring for the first time to a countable noun, and "the" for subsequent references.
i. We use "the" with singular countable nouns to make general statements.
j. We can use "the" plus an adjective to denote a group of people.
k. We use no article when we are referring to the usual function of an institution.

GRAMMAR – STUDY SHEET 7

Essay correction and analysis

An intermediate level student has been asked to write a description (given below), using direct and reported speech, of a time when he had returned a purchase to a shop with a complaint. He had been briefed to write it in three parts:

- The scene setting, using mainly the simple past tense
- The dialogue, in direct speech
- The follow-up to the dialogue and end of the story, using reported speech

Task:

a. *Verbs: considering the aim of the exercise (direct and reported speech, see Appendix and Swan, Sections 274-278, 474.6; Appendix, Study Sheet 7)* **list the main verb errors which you feel you should focus on as a teacher. State exactly the verb tense which the student has used, and the form he should have used.**

b. **Now look at the verbs, and under the grammar points which he has used <u>correctly</u>, and state which forms he appears to be in full command of.**

c. **Comment on other grammatical, lexical or orthographical areas which you feel you would focus on in future lessons.**

"One day wandering in London, I saw in the Curry's windowshop a few ipod's. I was supprised (sic) by the prices, then I decided to look for some others shop to compare the prices, my first impression was the good one the Curry's prices were the cheapest and even cheaper than the Frenchs prices. So I decided to buy one thinking It (sic) was a good value for money. it (sic) was a 4th generation I was very proud of my purchase. But when I as (sic) back home, It appeared that the ipod didn't work in fact it didn't reverse. Angry I return to the shop to have my money back.
I came into the shop and had for the salesman, and said.
-"I bought this ipod two hours before, and It (sic) do not work"
-"It's not possible" said the salesman and he added "what's wrong with it"
-"It doesn't rewind. So I want my money back" I claimed
-"I'm sorry it's not possible, the best I can do It's to give you a new one"
-"I don't want a new one, I want my money back let me see the manager please". I said.
Finally the manager came and explained to me the same thing, I can have my money back, but he can change my purchase against a new one, but I didn't accept this so I answered this that I would be going to complain of it at a customers organisation. When he heard this, he changed his mind, and claimed that he would be going to give me my money back, but It was the first time he did it, and just because he didn't record this purchase in his account yet".

CELTA Grammar & Pronunciation Study Pack by Pamela Benson ©2017

PRONUNCIATION – STUDY GUIDE page 1

Being aware of English Pronunciation

Key vocabulary

sentence stress
shifting/variable stress
pitch
contraction
syllable

rhythm
intonation
weak form
unmarked form

Your experience as a learner

Think about your experience as a language learner. If possible, choose an experience which happened to you as an adult learner. Try to answer these questions:

- Were you helped to "hear" the new sounds of the language before you were asked to reproduce them? How?
- If you couldn't reproduce the sounds, were you given corrective help? How?
- Were you aware or made aware of how close or how far your pronunciation was from the target language? Were you given any feedback as to the progress of your pronunciation?
- What was highest in your priority rating-accuracy in grammar and vocabulary, or accuracy in pronunciation?
- Why were you learning the target language? What goals did you set yourself? Did you achieve them?
- How satisfactory was the learning experience?

Now write a short description on Answer Sheet 1.

PRONUNCIATION – STUDY GUIDE page 2

Word stress
(Swan, Section 554)

We recognise English words not only by their sounds but by their stress pattern. Thus the verb "export" and the noun "export" have different stress patterns. The verb has the second syllable stressed "ex**port**", and the noun has the first syllable "**ex**port".

It is important when teaching new words of more than one syllable, to point out and practise their particular stress pattern.
There are several methods for noting stress patterns. We focus here on two. Approach them as follows:

There are several methods for noting stress patterns. We focus here on two A or B. Approach them as follows:

1. By saying the word aloud, decide how many syllables there are, and where they begin and end:

    ex.port = 2 syllables;   ex.port.ed = 3 syllables

2. Say the word aloud again, and decide which has the most stress:

    ex.port = first syllable;   ex.**port**.ed = second syllable

Then, Method A:

Write the word either with a small vertical mark <u>in front of</u> the stressed syllable, or with a large syllable above the stressed syllable.

      O   O
  ex'port;   ex'ported

Add small circles for the other syllables:

    O o   o O o
  ex'port;   ex'ported

Or, Method B:

Write the word with a small vertical mark in front of the stressed syllable.

You may find Method A, the small and large circle useful for classroom board work, but Method B is common in EFL dictionaries. So it's best to be familiar with both methods. Method B requires more precision in determining where the syllables begin and end.

CELTA Grammar & Pronunciation Study Pack by Pamela Benson ©2017

PRONUNCIATION – STUDY GUIDE page 3

Note: If you are in doubt about syllabic division, you can refe9r to an EFL dictionary such as *Oxford Advanced Learners Dictionary,* the *Longman Dictionary* or *Collins Cobuild,* and check which system they use. It's as well to become very familiar with at least one of these EFL learner dictionaries (all are available in softback).

Example: *The Oxford Advanced Learners Dictionary*

as.sig.na.tion = showing its spelling, and possible division points: this word can be divided as "assign-nation" or "assigna-tion", etc. Each language has its own rules for end-of-line word division, and when contravened, predicting the word to follow becomes more difficult for the reader.

So in this word "assignation" the primary stress falls on the third syllable, the secondary stress falls on the first syllable.

Now work through Answer Sheet 3.

Rhythm – unmarked form
(Swan, Section 554.6)

We have learned that polysyllabic words contain their own stress pattern, which is as much a feature of the word as their spoken sound and their spelling.

When words are put together into a sentence, the pattern of stressed and unstressed syllables creates a tum-titty-tum effect. Swan notes that within an utterance such as a sentence, strong beats fall on certain types of words, called content words and weak beats on other types of words, called function words. An example:

She was SURE that the BACK of the CAR had been DAMAGED.

The stress falls on the adjective 'sure', on the nouns 'back', 'car', and the first syllable of the main verb 'damaged'.

Now work through Answer Sheet 5.

Sentence stress – marked form
(Swan, 554)

We have seen that certain types of words tend to be stressed more than other types of words, in the unmarked utterance (an utterance without any special emphasis). When the speaker wishes to make a particular point, they might use the same sentence, but give extra weighting to one or more words, thus changing the emphasis. Thus:

"He likes travelling by car"   =   unmarked form, a pure statement of fact

"He **likes** travelling by car"   =   extra stress on "likes", possibly to correct the listener who thought Tom didn't like travelling by car

"He likes travelling by **car**"   =   extra stress on "car", possibly to contrast the other forms of transport he dislikes.

A precise interpretation of sentence stress can only be made with knowledge of the context in which it is said.

Now write three pairs of sentences illustrating sentence stress, on Answer Sheet 6. Make sure all the words are underlined which normally take a stress, plus the emphasised word.

PRONUNCIATION – STUDY GUIDE page 5

Weak forms
(Swan, 554)

It is important for the teacher, not only to encourage the students to be aware of words which can have a strong and a weak form, but also to be careful, when speaking slowly, i.e. when dictating, or when saying words in isolation, not to use the strong form in isolation, when a weak form is said in its usual spoken context.

Reread the relevant sections note above of Swan.

Now work on the bottom half of Answer Sheet 6.

Optional further reading

<u>English Phonetics and Phonology</u>, Peter Roach, second edition, Cambridge University Press, Reprinted 2009.

VARIETIES OF ENGLISH — STUDY SHEET

You can attempt this section relying on your background knowledge and understanding. However, it would be your advantage to complete the Answer Sheet after a careful reading of Chapters 1-4 of *Varieties of English*. There are a number of grammatical terms in the text: regular and irregular verbs; transitive and intransitive verbs; pronouns (relative, subject, object, demonstrative, possessive and reflexive), etc. If you have read the Swan text, and completed the Answer Sheets, you should be familiar with the terminology. If you are unclear, refer back to Swan using the index at the back of the book.

The aim of reading this text, a of completing the Answer Sheet, is to increase your understanding of the varieties of English to be found in the British Isles, and to be more aware of the origin and scope of the variety of English taught in the EFL classroom. Along the way, you will hopefully get some insights into the English which you yourself speak, and with which you come into contact.

Each of us has been brought up with a set of ideas relating to what good English is. The book asks you to look afresh in a descriptive rather prescriptive manner.

GRAMMAR   ANSWER SHEET 1

Task:
Referring o Swan, Section 10, list one or more examples of the following verb tenses and verb types to be found in the passage "Island Paradise". Please include the subjects of the verbs you select.

1. Present Simple

2. Present continuous

3. Future simple

4. Present perfect active

5. Present perfect passive

6. Past perfect

7. Simple past active

8. Simple past passive

9. Infinitive

10. Present participle

11. Past participle

12. Modal verb

GRAMMAR   ANSWER SHEET 2

A. Task:

Label the verb tenses below, and mark the correct constituent part analysis (listed on the study sheet) for each verb tense. Note that a particular form may be applicable more than once.

Example

He walks
    Tense: present simple
    Formed of: d

1. He finished
    Tense _____

    Formed of: _____

2. He has eaten
    Tense _____

    Formed of: _____

3. He has been working
    Tense _____

    Formed of: _____

4. He has been conned
    Tense _____

    Formed of: _____

5. He had escaped
    Tense _____

    Formed of: _____

6. He had been hoping
    Tense _____

    Formed of: _____

7. He had been conned
    Tense _____

    Formed of: _____

8. He will remember
    Tense _____

    Formed of: _____

9. He will be travelling
    Tense _____

    Formed of: _____

10. He will have been trying
    Tense _____

    Formed of: _____

11. He will have been rescued
    Tense _____

    Formed of: _____

12. He might have been disappointed
    Tense _____

    Formed of: _____

GRAMMAR   ANSWER SHEET 3

Each sentence contains a wrong use of a verb tense.

    A. Task:

    a. correct the error, i.e. rewrite the sentence
    b. name the incorrect verb tense
    c. name the correct verb tense
    d. comment briefly on the use of the correct tense, referring to the relevant part of Swan.

Example: "I am here since 1900."

    a. I have been here since 2000
    b. present simple of verb to be
    c. present perfect of verb to be
    d. present perfect use with an action that started at an unspecified time in the past and which continues into the present. Swan, Sections 460/463.

1. "I will tell him about it when we will meet."

    a. _____
    b. _____
    c. _____
    d. _____

2. "I am smoking 20 cigarettes a day."

    a. _____
    b. _____
    c. _____
    d. _____

3. "He has left his country 2 years ago."

   a. _____
   b. _____
   c. _____
   d. _____

4. "She already ate breakfast when the post arrived."

   a. _____
   b. _____
   c. _____
   d. _____

5. "I have lived in London for 2 years."

   a. _____
   b. _____
   c. _____
   d. _____

6. "She had a bath when the phone rang."

   a. _____
   b. _____
   c. _____
   d. _____

7. "I smoked cigarettes ever since I can remember."

a. _____

b. _____

c. _____

d. _____

GRAMMAR   ANSWER SHEET 3 cont.

B. **Task: write a brief paragraph discussing points 8 an 9 below:**

8. A student asks why they can't abbreviate: "He's an athletic build", when they can abbreviate both: "He's got an athletic build", and "He's an athlete". What is the reason? Can you think of other examples to illustrate this point?

9. A student who recently visited Windsor Castle writes "I'm really glad that we have been to Windsor Castle". Another student asks "Which verb is this? Shouldn't it be 'We've gone to Windsor Castle?'" What do you reply?

C. **Task: Give an explanation of the meaning of each a and b, which focuses on the difference in meaning. Refer to the relevant part of Swan.**

10a. "I **used to** go camping"
10b. "I **am used to** camping"

a. _____

b. _____

c. Reference
_____

GRAMMAR   ANSWER SHEET 4

Task: Regular and irregular verbs

Write the past tense and 7 past participle forms of the following verbs, and decide which verb type they fall into: type b, two forms; or type c, three forms. If necessary, refer to a dictionary. If a verb has two possible forms for one tense, list both.

	Base form	simple past tense	past participle	type
Example	bite	bit	bitten	c
1.	cut			
2.	burn			
3.	become			
4.	outbid			
5.	lay			
6.	lie			
7.	arise			
8.	beat			
9.	be			
10.	dream			

Transitive and intransitive verbs

Task:

Refer to Swan, Section 606 and check you understand what these terms mean. Then identify the verbs underlined in the following sentences as either transitive: vt, or intransitive: vi. Don't forget that some verbs are either one or the other, while others can be used in both ways. Take the verb as used in the sentence. Be careful with passives, and with phrasal verbs.

Example: Prices dropped in the summer   vi
            He dropped the plate   vt

1. He eats bananas but not kiwis   _____
2. He does nothing but eat   _____
3. She rose at dawn   _____
4. The flag was raised at dawn   _____
5. The boy lay down to sleep   _____
6. He laid the book on the table   _____
7. He dropped the eggs in Tesco   _____
8. His face dropped at the mention of homework   _____
9. She ran the length of the hall   _____
10. She ran the risk of offending her boss   _____

GRAMMAR   ANSWER SHEET 5

Task 1. Conditionals (Refer to Swan, Section 257-259 and *Appendix, Grammar Study Sheet 5*)

Reorder the following sentences into three main conditional types. State the verb tenses used for the underlined verbs. The tenses are: past perfect, present form of would, present simple, future, past form of would, simple past. (See Swan, Section, 264)

If I <u>enjoyed</u> parachuting, I <u>would do</u> it again.
If I <u>enjoy</u> parachuting, <u>I will do</u> it again.
If I <u>had enjoyed</u> parachuting, I <u>would have done</u> it again.

1a   1st Type
       Tenses:

1b   2nd Type
       Tenses:

1c   3rd Type
       Tenses:

Many conditional sentences are based on a "suppose". The conditional sentence is contrary to fact. For example, "If I wanted, I could learn Somali", the fact is I don't want to learn Somali.

Look at the "fact" sentences below, and decide which of the conditional types listed above, they relate to.

                                                                                            Conditional type

1d. One refers to the future. I haven't been parachuting yet. It is a
possibility that I will enjoy it.   _____

1e. One refers to a past experience of parachuting and I hated it and
turned down the offer of doing it again.   _____

1f. One makes a general statement about my feelings about parachuting.
It is unclear whether I have been or not. To say I enjoy it would be
Untrue and it is doubtful I will do it again.   _____

Now write the corresponding conditional sentences and say which types of conditional you have used: 1st, 2nd and 3rd Types, 3, or mixed, and give reasons. (Refer to 1d, e, f, as a guide).

    2. Fact: I ate the pizza and I felt sick

    Conditional: _____

    Type: _____

    Reason: _____

CELTA Grammar & Pronunciation Study Pack by Pamela Benson ©2017

3. Fact: I ate the pizza and I feel sick.

   Conditional: _____

   Type: _____

   Reason: _____

4. Fact: He smokes a lot and has difficulty breathing.

   Conditional: _____

   Type: _____

   Reason: _____

5. Fact: The children are playing happily and she doesn't have a camera!

   Conditional: _____

   Type: _____

   Reason: _____

6. Fact: He has an interview next week and he can't decide whether to go by coach or train.

   Conditional: _____

   Type: _____

   Reason: _____

GRAMMAR   ANSWER SHEET 6

Articles

Task:

Select and mark the "rule of use" which best explains the use, or omission of the article.

Example:

1. I always like to have a drink before going to bed.
   Rule of use: c

2. The radio he gave me is a Sony.
   Rule of use: ____

3. Vegetarians don't eat meat.
   Rule of use: ____

4. The car has become a status symbol.
   Rule of use: ____

5. Life in developing countries can be hard.
   Rule of use: ____

6. The life I lead is full of surprises.
   Rule of use: ____

7. Blessed are the poor, for they shall inherit the earth.
   Rule of use: ____

8. Once there lived an old man in a cottage. The old man was very poor.
   Rule of use: ____

9. Put the vase on the piano, it looks nice there.
   Rule of use: ____

10. I'm an astronaut, my husband's a nurse.
    Rule of use: ____

11. I'm going to the post office.
    Rule of use: ____

12. The Earth is not flat as we once thought, nor is the moon made of cheese.
    Rule of use: ____

13. She's at school today.
    Rule of use: ____

14. I'm going to a parents meeting at the school.
    Rule of use: ____

GRAMMAR ANSWER SHEET 7

Essay correction and analysis

Task:
Analyse the student essay printed on the study sheet. Write your analysis under the headings a-c, given on the Study sheet.

Continue on the other side of the sheet and additional blank sheets, if necessary.

PRONUNCIATION — ANSWER SHEET 1

Your experience as a learner

Task:
Write a short description of your experience as a language learner. If possible, choose an experience which happened to you as an adult learner. Try to answer the questions in the Study Guide.

PRONUNCIATION   Answer Sheet 2

Task:
Read these words loud and note where the stress falls, using the two methods discussed in the study sheet.

                            O   o
Example: transport   transport

bauxite   _____   Parmesan   _____

confession   _____   perquisite   _____

foolhardy   _____   persevere   _____

extraordinary _____   septicaemia   _____

ungovernable _____   kettle-drum   _____

Task:
Identify the unstressed syllable in each of these words (some may have more than one), by underlining the corresponding vowel letter.

underlined unstressed syllables

example:
dialogue   di<u>a</u>logue

survive
offend
forbid
sullen
vicious
yesterday
hundred
workaday
photograph
photographer
perjury
ballad
borough
percent
major

CELTA Grammar & Pronunciation Study Pack by Pamela Benson ©2017

PRONUNCIATION — ANSWER SHEET 3

Task: Rhythm

Note where the strong beat falls in these sentences and:

a. Mark it by underlining the word. (Don't worry about which syllable within the word is stressed, just underline the words in the sentence with one stressed).
b. Rewrite it as a "da DA da" sentence (one syllable for each "da").
c. Write large Das as large O, and small das as small o, underneath the "beat" it represents.
d. Note which type of words have the "strong beat".

Example:
   a. There isn't any salt on the table
   b. da DA da da da DA da da DA da
   c. o O o o o O o o O o
   d. verb, noun, noun

1. I travel to school by bus.
   a. _____
   b. _____
   c. _____
   d. _____

2. He went to America and never came back.
   a. _____
   b. _____
   c. _____
   d. _____

3. I wish you wouldn't grin at me like that!
   a. _____
   b. _____
   c. _____
   d. _____

4. I can't stand green bananas!
   e. _____
   f. _____
   g. _____
   h. _____

3. She's a really keen potholer.
   a. _____
   b. _____
   c. _____
   d. _____

Task:
Write the rhythm of this dialogue, using the large O and a small o to mark the strong and weak beat, as used in the text.

Example: O o   O o O   o   O o
   "Dinner's ready. Come and get it. "

_____

"Have you ever been to Salisbury?" (note: only two syllables in Salisbury)

_____

"No, I haven't."

_____

"Would you like to come with me?"

_____

"Sure, that would be lovely."

PRONUNCIATION — ANSWER SHEET 4

Task: Sentence stress

Write three pairs of sentences, each with different sentence stress. Mark out the strong beats with one underline, the emphasis with double underlines, as in the Study Guide. Write a possible interpretation underneath each sentence.

1a _____
= _____
1b _____
= _____
2a _____
= _____
2b _____
= _____
3a _____
= _____
3b _____
= _____

Task: Weak forms

Read the following text aloud, at normal speed, and underline the words which are pronounced with a weak form.

Brazil has a population of 210 million, and it is growing at a rate of 2.3 per cent a year. If this continues there will be 600 million by the year 2050.

With this large number of mouths to feed, and bodies to clothe, many people in Brazil get left behind. 45 million people live in poverty today, any of whom suffer from malnutrition or are abandoned by their parents. Birth control is not effectively promoted by the government, due to opposition from the Roman Catholic Church, and bureaucratic inefficiency.

Brazilian society is built on a pyramidic structure. At the top are a few rich "have-a-lot"s, then lower down on the next level, the middle class "have-enough"s, then at the bottom, at the base of the pyramid, the millions of poor "don't-have-enough"s.

VARIETIES — ANSWER SHEET 1

Task: Accent and dialect

Write a paragraph on each of the topics below:

a. Write a short description of what you now understand by: accent/regional accent, and dialect/regional accent.
b. What do you understand *Received Pronunciation* and *Standard English* to be?
c. Referring specifically to the variety of English you yourself speak, and varieties within your family/work/social context, try to label the language you use and with which you come into contact.
d. Is it true to say that *Standard English* was and is a prestige dialect?

GRAMMAR　　　　　　　　　　　　　　ANSWERS 1A

Task:
Referring to Swan, Section 10, list one or more examples of the following verb tenses and verb types to be found in the passage "Spaceship Earth". Please include the subjects of the verbs you select.

1. Present simple which contains, you breathe, you eat, you drink, you wash, it provides, new people arrive, no one seems, breaks up etc. **2. Present continuous** you are living, food and water isn't getting to, others are claiming, the fighting is unbalancing, the quality is deteriorating. **3. Future simple** there will be, will he say. **4. Present perfect active** the inhabitants have begun, fighting has caused. **5. Present perfect passive** the number has been reached, many resources have been finished, supplies have been used up. **6. Past perfect** the commander had estimated. **7. Past simple active** the island had, the inhabitants arrived, the life forms were, the inhabitants got on with.	**8. Past simple passive** was thought, below were buried. **9. Infinitive** to survive, to forget, , to realise, to have, to behave, to make, etc. **10. Present participle** Following, being **11. Past participle** worried, grown, been, done, caused, isolated, furnished, buried. **12. Modal verb** <u>might</u> hold, food <u>can</u> be grown, something <u>must</u> be done, it <u>should</u> have been done.

GRAMMAR   ANSWERS 2a

Verb tenses: constituent parts

A. Task
Label the verb tenses below, and mark the correct constituent part analysis (listed on the study sheet) for each verb tense. Note that a particular form may be applicable more than once.

Example

He walks

    Tense: present simple
    Formed of: d

1. He finished
       Tense: simple past (active)

       Formed of: ____f____

2. He has eaten
       Tense: present perfect (simple) (active)

       Formed of: ____k____

3. He has been working
       Tense: present perfect continuous (active)

       Formed of: ____b____

4. He has been conned
       Tense: present perfect (simple) active

       Formed of: ____e____

5. He had escaped
       Tense: past perfect (simple) (active)

       Formed of: ____l____

6. He had been hoping
    Tense: present perfect continuous (active)

    Formed of: ____a____

7. He had been conned
    Tense: present perfect (simple) passive

    Formed of: ____j____

8. He will remember
    Tense: future simple

    Formed of: ____h____

9. He will be travelling
    Tense: future continuous

    Formed of: ____g____

10. He will have been trying
    Tense: future perfect continuous

    Formed of: ____i____

11. He will have been rescued
    Tense: future perfect passive

    Formed of: ____c____

12. He might have been disappointed
    Tense: passive form of 'might'   (i.e. might and passive infinitive)

    Formed of: ____c____

GRAMMAR   ANSWERS 3a

Each sentence contains a wrong use of a verb tense.

   A. **Task:**

   e. *correct the error, i.e. rewrite the sentence*
   f. *name the incorrect verb tense*
   g. *name the correct verb tense*
   h. *comment briefly on the use of the correct tense, referring to the relevant part of Swan.*

Example: "I am here since 1900."

   a. I have been here since 2000
   b. present simple of verb to be
   c. present perfect of verb to be
   d. present perfect use with an action that started at an unspecified time in the past and which continues into the present. Swan, Section 460/463.

1. "I will tell him about it when we will meet."
   a. I will tell him about it when we meet.
   b. future simple of verb to meet
   c. present simple of verb to meet
   d. In a time clause referring to the future, the verb in the subordinate clause (after the conjunction 'when') is in the present tense. Swan, Section 580.2.

2. "I am smoking 20 cigarettes a day"
   a. I smoke 20 cigarettes a day.
   b. present continuous of verb to smoke
   c. present simple of verb to smoke
   d. The present simple is used to express an action that is a routine, a habit. Swan, Section 465.

3. "He has left his country two years ago"
   a. He left his country two years ago.
   b. present perfect tense of verb to leave
   c. simple past tense of verb to leave
   d. The simple past is used when referring to a competed action and definite point of time in the past. Swan, Section 421.

4. "She already ate breakfast when the post arrived"
   a. She had already eaten breakfast when the post arrived.

CELTA Grammar & Pronunciation Study Pack by Pamela Benson ©2017

      b. simple past of verb to eat
      c. past perfect of verb to eat
      d. The past perfect is used to describe and action that happened before another action in the past. Swan, Section 423

5. "I have lived in London for two years"
      a. I lived in London for two years
      b. present perfect of verb to live
      c. simple past of verb to live
      d. The simple past is used when referring to a completed action and a period of time in the past which have no connection with the present. Swan, Section 421.

6. "She had a bath when the phone rang"
      a. She was having a bath when the phone rang
      b. simple past of verb to have
      c. past continuous of verb to have
      d. The past continuous is used here to describe an action in the past that started before and was interrupted by another one. Swan, Section 422.

7. "I smoked cigarettes ever since I can remember"
      a. I have smoked cigarettes ever since I can remember
      b. Simple past of verb to smoke
      c. Present perfect of verb to smoke
      d. The present perfect is used here to describe an action that started at an Indefinite time in the past and continues into the present. Swan, Section 455.

GRAMMAR   ANSWERS 3A cont.

D. Task: write a brief paragraph discussing points 8 an 9 below:

10. A student asks why they can't abbreviate: "He's an athletic build", when they can abbreviate both: "He's got an athletic build", and "He's an athlete". What is the reason? Can you think of other examples to illustrate this point?

> When' to have' is a main verb it cannot be abbreviated.
> 'He's an athletic build' should be 'He has an athletic build'
> When 'to have' is an auxiliary verb it can be abbreviated.
> 'He's got an athletic build' = 'He has got an athletic build'. Both are correct.
> He's an athlete = He is an athlete.
> The verb 'to be' can always be abbreviated.
> He has an artistic temperament. He's got an artistic temperament. He's an artist.

11. A student who recently visited Windsor Castle writes "I'm really glad that we have been to Windsor Castle". Another student asks "Which verb is this? Shouldn't it be 'We've gone to Windsor Castle?'" What do you reply?

> We've been (verb to be) implies speaker has been away visiting a place and come back.
> We've gone (verb to go) implies the speaker is still away visiting a place.
> Since the student is writing about the complete experience, the sentence 'we've been' is correct.
> 'We've gone would mean he was still at Windsor Castle.
> Swan, Section 94

E. Task: Give an explanation of the meaning of each a and b, which focuses on the difference in meaning. Refer to the relevant part of Swan.

10a. "I **used to** go camping"
10b. "I **am used to** camping"

a. I camped a number of times or regularly in the past but no longer do so: regular action is discontinued.

 Camping is something I do currently and I am accustomed to it.

d. Reference   Swan, Section 605.

GRAMMAR – ANSWERS 4A

Regular and irregular verbs

Task:

Students learn irregular verbs (sometimes called "strong" verbs, but not usually by ESL teachers) by heart, and expect the teacher to instantly recite their three essential forms!

Write the simple past tense and past participle forms of the following verbs, and decide which verb type they fall into:

Type a, one form only;   type b, two forms;   or type c, three forms

If necessary, refer to a dictionary. If a verb has two possible forms for one tense, list both.

	Base form	simple past tense	past participle	type
Example	bite	bit	bitten	c
1.	cut	cut	cut	a
2.	burn	burn	burn	b
3.	become	became	became	b
4.	outbid	outbid(ded)	outbid(ded)	a/b
5.	lay	laid	laid	b
6.	lie	lay	lain	c
7.	arise	arose	arisen	c
8.	beat	beat	beaten	b
9.	be	was	been	c
10.	dream	dreamt/ed	dreamt/ed	b

Transitive and intransitive verbs

Task:

Refer to Swan, Section 606 and check you understand what these terms mean. Then identify the verbs underlined in the following sentences as either transitive: vt, or intransitive: vi. Don't forget that some verbs are either one or the other, while others can be used in both ways. Take the verb as used in the sentence. Be careful with passives, and with phrasal verbs.

Example: Prices dropped in the summer   vi
          He dropped the plate   vt

1. He eats bananas but not kiwis   vt
2. He does nothing but eat   vi
3. She rose at dawn   vi
4. The flag was raised at dawn   vt
5. The boy lay down to sleep   vi
6. He laid the book on the table   vt
7. He dropped the eggs in Tesco   vt
8. His face dropped at the mention of homework   vi
9. She ran the length of the hall   vi
10. She ran the risk of offending her boss   vt

GRAMMAR   ANSWERS 5

Task 1. Conditionals (Refer to Swan, Section 259-261)

Reorder the following sentences into three main conditional types. State the verb tenses used for the underlined verbs. The tenses are: past perfect, present form of would, present simple, future, past form of would, simple past. (See Swan, Section, 141.1, 258.6 – 26)

If I enjoyed parachuting, I would do it again.
If I enjoy parachuting, I will do it again.
If I had enjoyed parachuting, I would have done it again.

1a   Type 1
     Tenses: present simple, future simple

1b   Type 2
     Tenses: simple past, present form of would

1c   Type 3
     Tenses: past perfect, past form of would

Many conditional sentences are based on a "suppose". The conditional sentence is contrary to fact. For example, "If I wanted, I could learn Somali", the fact is I don't want to learn Somali.

Look at the "fact" sentences below, and decide which of the conditional types listed above, they relate to.

                                                                    Conditional type

1d. One refers to the future. I haven't been parachuting yet. It is a
possibility that I will enjoy it.   ___1___

1e. One refers to a past experience of parachuting and I hated it and
turned down the offer of doing it again.   ___3___

1f. One makes a general statement about my feelings about parachuting.
It is unclear whether I have been or not. To say I enjoy it would be
Untrue and it is doubtful I will do it again.   ___2___

Now write the corresponding conditional sentences and say which types of conditional you have used: Types 1, 2, 3, or mixed, and give reasons. (Refer to 1d, e, f, as a guide).

   2. Fact: I ate the pizza and I felt sick

      Conditional: If I hadn't eaten the pizza, I wouldn't have felt sick.

      Type: 3

      Reason: Refers to action that happened in the past (a regret).

3. Fact: I ate the pizza and I feel sick.

   Conditional: If I hadn't eaten the pizza, I wouldn't be feeling/feel sick.

   Type: Mixed: 3 and 2

   Reason: I ate the pizza in the past, but I feel sick now, i.e. past action with result or consequence of it in the present.

4. Fact: He smokes a lot and has difficulty breathing.

   Conditional: If he didn't smoke too much he wouldn't have difficulty breathing.

   Type: 2

   Reason: Refers to a current action in the present (a complaint).

5. Fact: The children are playing happily and she doesn't have a camera!

   Conditional: If (only) she had a camera, she could take their picture.

   Type: 2

   Reason: Refers to an action in the present. Could is substituted for 'would'.

6. Fact: He has an interview next week and he can't decide whether to go by coach or train.

   Conditional: If he goes by   train, it will be faster but more expensive.
                                 coach, it will be slower but cheaper.

   Type: 1

   Reason: Refers to a specified future time.

GRAMMAR   **ANSWERS 6A**

Articles
Task:
Select and mark the "rule of use" which best explains the use, or omission of the article.

Example:

1. I always like to have a drink before going to bed.
   Rule of use: c

2. The radio he gave me is a Sony.
   Rule of use: __a__

3. Vegetarians don't eat meat.
   Rule of use: __g__

4. The car has become a status symbol.
   Rule of use: __i__

5. Life in developing countries can be hard.
   Rule of use: __b__

6. The life I lead is full of surprises.
   Rule of use: __a__

7. Blessed are the poor, for they shall inherit the earth.
   Rule of use: __i__

8. Once there lived an old man in a cottage. The old man was very poor.
   Rule of use: __h__

9. Put the vase on the piano, it looks nice there.
   Rule of use: __a/d__

10. I'm an astronaut, my husband's a nurse.
    Rule of use: __e__

11. I'm going to the post office.
    Rule of use: __d__

12. The Earth is not flat as we once thought, nor is the moon made of cheese.
    Rule of use: _a/i/d_

13. She's at school today.
    Rule of use: __k__

14. I'm going to a parents meeting at the school.
    Rule of use: _f/d_

GRAMMAR   ANSWERS 7A

Essay correction and analysis

Task:
Analyse the student essay printed on the study sheet. Write your analysis under the headings a-c, given on the Study sheet.

Continue on the other side of the sheet and additional blank sheets, if necessary.

You should make mention of these:
a)
    1. 'return' (present simple) should be 'returned' (past simple).
    2. 'head' (present simple) should be 'headed' (past simple).
    3. 'can't have my money' (present simple) should be 'couldn't' (past).
    4. 'I will be going to complain' ('going to' form of future added) should be 'I would complain' (past of 'will').
    5. 'he would be going to give' ('going to' form of future added) should be 'he would give' (past of 'will'). 3,4,5, all correct forms follow the rules of reported speech.
    6. 'he did it' (simple past) should be 'he had done it' (past perfect)
    7. 'he didn't record' (simple past) should be 'he hadn't recorded it'.
    8. I answered him. No pronoun necessary here. I answered + direct speech or I replied that + indirect speech.

b). You should refer to   shortened forms: it's, doesn't, don't (exception: it do not work) he used inverted commas correctly
    he uses capital letters correctly at the beginning of a sentence (exception: 'I' in the middle.

Apart from verbs in a) he knows correct spelling of verbs = past tenses.
Plus – comparatives: 'even cheaper than'
Present participles – wandering, thinking

c). You should isolate these areas:
Rules of reported speech, See a)
Plurals and adjectives describing plural forms: walkman's
                                            others shop
                                            Frenchs

Definite and indefinite articles:
    the good one
    a good value
    the Curry's

Vocabulary and spelling: window shop
                                  supprised

These are the main areas. There are lots of incidental mistakes that need to be corrected and revised: charge something for, not against.
Complain about something to someone, not of something at someone.

CELTA Grammar & Pronunciation Study Pack by Pamela Benson ©2017

PRONUNCIATION — ANSWERS 1A

Your experience as a learner

Task:
Write a short description of your experience as a language learner. If possible, choose an experience which happened to you as an adult learner. Try to answer the questions in the Study Guide.

PRONUNCIATION   ANSWERS 2A

Task:
Read these words loud and note where the stress falls, using the two methods discussed in the study sheet.

Example: transport   O o
                         transport

bauxite	O o bauxite	Parmesan	o o O O o o Parmesan, Parmesan
confession	o O o confession	perquisite	O o o perquisite
foolhardy	O o o foolhardy	persevere	o o O persevere
extraordinary	o O o o extraordinary	septicaemia	o o O o septicemia
ungovernable	o O o o ungovernable	kettle-drum	O o o kettle-drum

Task: Unstressed syllables
Identify the unstressed syllable in each of these words (some may have more than one), by underlining the corresponding vowel letter.

underlined unstressed syllables

example:
dialogue   di<u>a</u>logue

survive   s<u>u</u>rvive
offend   <u>o</u>ffend
forbid   f<u>o</u>rbid
sullen   sull<u>e</u>n
vicious   vici<u>ou</u>s
yesterday   yest<u>e</u>rday
hundred   hundr<u>e</u>d
workaday   work<u>a</u>day
photograph   phot<u>o</u>graph
photographer   ph<u>o</u>togr<u>a</u>ph<u>e</u>r
perjury   perj<u>u</u>ry
ballad   ball<u>a</u>d
borough   bor<u>o</u>ugh
percent   p<u>e</u>rcent
major   maj<u>o</u>r

PRONUNCIATION — ANSWERS 3A

Task: Rhythm

Note where the strong beat falls in these sentences and:

e. Mark it by underlining the word. (Don't worry about which syllable within the word is stressed, just underline the words in the sentence with one stressed).
f. Rewrite it as a "da DA da" sentence (one syllable for each "da").
g. Write large Das as large O, and small das as small o, underneath the "beat" it represents.
h. Note which type of words have the "strong beat".

Example:
   a. There <u>isn't</u> any <u>salt</u> on the <u>table</u>
   b. da DA da da da DA da da DA da
   c. o O o o o O o o O o
   d.   verb   noun   noun

1. I travel to school by bus.
   a. I <u>travel</u> to <u>school</u> by <u>bus</u>.
   b. da DA da da DA da DA
   c. o O o o O o O
   d.   verb   noun   noun

2. He <u>went</u> to A<u>me</u>rica and <u>never</u> came <u>back</u>.
   a. He went to America and never came back.
   b. da DA da da DA da da da DA da da DA
   c. o O o o O o o o O o o O
   d.   verb   noun   adverb   adverb

3. I <u>wish</u> you <u>wouldn't</u> <u>grin</u> at me like <u>that</u>!
   a. I wish you wouldn't grin at me like that!
   b. da DA da da DA da da da DA
   c. o O o o O o o o O
   d.   verb   noun   pronoun

4. I can't <u>stand</u> green ba<u>na</u>nas!
   a. I can't stand green bananas!
   b. da da DA da da DA da
   c. o o O o o O o
   e.   verb   noun

3. She's a <u>really</u> <u>keen</u> <u>pot</u>holer.
   a. She's a really keen potholer.
   b. da da DA da DA DA da da
   c. o o O o O O o o
   d.   adverb adjective noun

Task:
Write the rhythm of this dialogue, using the large O and a small o to mark the strong and weak beat, as used in the text.

Example: O o   O o O   o   O o
                 "Dinner's ready. Come and get it."

  o   o O o   o   o O   o
"Have you ever been to Salisbury?" (note: only two syllables in Salisbury)

  O o O o
"No, I haven't."

    o   o O o O   o   O
"Would you like to come with me?" ('come' is optional stress)

   O   O   o   o O o
"Sure, that would be lovely."

CELTA Grammar & Pronunciation Study Pack by Pamela Benson ©2017

PRONUNCIATION — ANSWERS 4A

Task: Sentence stress

Write three pairs of sentences, , each with different sentence stress. Mark out the strong beats with one underline, the emphasis with double underlines, as in the Study Guide. Write a possible interpretation underneath each sentence.

1a I <u>like</u> <u>loo</u>king at <u>clo</u>thes in <u>Har</u>vey <u>Ni</u>chols
= unmarked form, a pure statement of fact
1b I <u>like</u> <u><u>loo</u></u>king at <u>clo</u>thes in <u>Har</u>vey <u>Ni</u>chols
= extra stress on "looking", conveying that that's as far as I go and don't buy them
2a _____
= _____
2b _____
= _____
3a _____
= _____
3b _____
= _____

Task: Weak forms

Read the following text aloud, at normal speed, and underline the words which are pronounced with a weak form.

Brazil <u>has</u> <u>a</u> population <u>of</u> 210 million, <u>and</u> <u>it</u> <u>is</u> growing <u>at</u> <u>a</u> rate <u>of</u> 2.3 per cent <u>a</u> year. If this continues there <u>will</u> <u>be</u> 600 million by <u>the</u> year 2050.

<u>With</u> this large number <u>of</u> mouths <u>to</u> feed, <u>and</u> bodies <u>to</u> clothe, many people <u>in</u> Brazil <u>get</u> left behind. 45 million people live <u>in</u> poverty today, any <u>of</u> whom suffer <u>from</u> malnutrition or <u>are</u> abandoned by <u>their</u> parents. Birth control <u>is</u> not effectively promoted by <u>the</u> government, due <u>to</u> opposition <u>from</u> <u>the</u> Roman Catholic Church, <u>and</u> bureaucratic inefficiency.

Brazilian society <u>is</u> built <u>on</u> <u>a</u> pyramidic structure. <u>At</u> <u>the</u> top <u>are</u> <u>the</u> few rich "have-<u>a</u>-lot"s, then lower down <u>on</u> <u>the</u> next level, <u>the</u> middle class "have-enough"s, then <u>at</u> <u>the</u> bottom, <u>at</u> <u>the</u> base <u>of</u> <u>the</u> pyramid, <u>the</u> millions <u>of</u> poor "don't-have-enough"s.

Some of the stresses are optional: stressing depends on <u>personal</u> speech patterns that vary in individuals.

VARIETIES   ANSWERS 1A

Task: Accent and dialect

Write a paragraph on each of the topics below:

a. Write a short description of what you now understand by: accent/regional accent, and dialect/regional accent.
b. What do you understand *Received Pronunciation* and *Standard English* to be?
c. Referring specifically to the variety of English you yourself speak, and varieties within your family/work/social context, try to label the language you use and with which you come into contact.
d. Is it true to say that *Standard English* was and is a prestige dialect?

a) Accent/regional accent

'Accent' refers to pronunciation. It is used to describe the pattern of sounds, inflections, stresses, etc., used in spoken language.
A regional accent is one used in a specific geographical region: an accent can be labelled 'American' because of certain recognisable pronunciation features Americans share.
Accent is also influenced be education, social class and gender.

Dialect/regional dialect

Dialect refers to a system of grammar and vocabulary used by a speaker/writer when it diverges from a perceived 'standard' form.
A regional dialect is a system of vocabulary and grammar shared by a people from a particular geographical region.
(A dialect retains sufficient words and structures in common with the 'standard' or other dialects for the general meaning of the language to be understood by people who use another dialect or the 'standard' language. At some point where this ceases to be the case it would be regarded as a separate, distinct language.)
Dialects are tending to disappear because of the influence of state education for all.

b) Received Pronunciation and Standard English

Received Pronunciation was the accent accepted and promoted by the BBC as the 'best' English which was believed to be understood by everyone. Broadly speaking, it was the accent of the educated, 'ruling' classes. The Pronunciation Unit within the BBC was set up to advise and determine what was the 'correct' pronunciation for the purposes of the BBC.

Nowadays, Received Pronunciation is accepted as a 'neutral' accent with no regional identity and, although it is still viewed by many as 'correct' or even 'educated (Southern) establishment' linguistically speaking, it is only one among many accents.

Standard English is a form of English whose grammar and vocabulary is recognised throughout the United Kingdom. Any deviations from it are recognised as regional variations or specialist lexis. Standard English is used when a commonly recognised language is necessary for public communication, and so it is used for the communication of news, instruction manuals, textbooks, 'official' press releases, everyday business communication, etc. Standard English is the form of language taught in schools and o speakers of other languages who wish to learn British English.

c) √

d) **Standard English is a prestige dialect.**

Briefly: socially and politically – yes; linguistically – no.

APPENDIX

GRAMMAR – STUDY SHEET 1

Twelve English Verb Tenses

1. **Present simple (routine, complicated actions, promises, instructions, stories, preferences, timetabled events)**
   I work, you work, he/she/it works, we work, they work

2. **Present continuous (situations around now, changes, the future, repeated actions, physical feelings)**
   I am working, you are working, etc

3. **Future simple (decisions, promises, offers, prediction)**
   I will/shall work, you will work, he/she/it will work, we will/shall work, they will work

4. **Present perfect active (person or thing that *does* the action) an action at an unspecified point in the past that affects now)**
   I have worked, you have worked, he/she/it has worked, etc

5. **Past perfect (an event which happened before another in the past)**
   I had worked, you had worked, he/she/it/had worked, etc

6. **Past simple active (a finished action in the past)**
   I worked, you worked, he/she/it worked, etc

7. **Past simple passive (person or thing *affected* by the finished action of the verb)**
   I was invited, your were invited, he/she/it was invited, etc*

8. **Infinitive (the base form of a verb)**
   (to) work, (to) be working, (to) have worked, (to) have been working

9. **Present perfect passive (person or thing *affected* by the continued action of the verb)**
   I have been approached, you have been approached, they have been approached, etc*

10. **Present participle (can be used with verb 'to be' to talk about past, present or future)**
    Working

11. **Past participle (can be used 'to be' to talk about past, present or future)**
    Worked

12. **Modal verb (used to *help* an main verb)**
    can. may, might, must, etc*

CELTA Grammar & Pronunciation Study Pack by Pamela Benson ©2017

GRAMMAR – STUDY SHEET 2

Verb Forms: *-ing* and *–ed*   Participles

- We can use the 'ing' for of verbs in certain ways. We call these 'present participles'. Other forms such as: *fallen, been, closed, finished* are known as 'past participles'. Despite the names, both can be used to talk about the past present or future.

    She was **laughing** with friends.   Who's he **talking** to?
    I'll be **seeing** him tomorrow night.
    My favourite team was **beaten**.   You're **drunk**!
    The leisure centre is going to be **improved**.

We can put present and past together to make continuous and perfect forms (being invited, having decided, having been rejected).

Auxiliary verbs *be* and *have* use participles to make continuous, perfect and passive verb forms.

    It **was snowing** when I arrived.   **I've lost** my bag.
    It**'ll be sold** soon.

- Participles can also be used as **adjectives**.

    I've just heard glass **breaking**.   He's got a **broken** leg.
    This is **interesting**.   The door was **closed**.

- Participles can also be used like **adverbs**.

    He came **walking** into the room.

- Participles can be combined with the words to produce semi-clause structures.

    Why is that woman **standing by the door**?

    Being late for the interview, I took a taxi.

    Most people **injured in the crash** went to hospital.

    Opened two weeks ago, the store is a great success.

GRAMMAR – STUDY SHEET 3

Used as an **adjective**. Verb *to be + used to*.
This means to be accustomed to.

For example:
I can study with noise around me. I am used to it. It means I am accustomed, adjusted, or don't mind noise around me.

Or: *Tim didn't like living in New York. He wasn't used to so many people.* Tim didn't have experience being with big crowds of people before.

Used as a verb. *Use to + verb* is a regular verb and means past habits or states that no longer exist. The *-ed* ending shows past tense. Since it always means that something took place in the past, it is always used in a past form.

For example:
I used to go to college in London. (I went to college there before, but now I don't.)

Or: *When Jane was a little girl, she used to have long hair.* (Now she doesn't have long hair.)

Remember, we always use this word when talking about the past. So when do you use *use to* without the *d* at the end? For questions and negative sentences the base form of the verb is used. Look at these examples:

She didn't use to eat before noon. (Now she eats before noon.)
Or *Did your father use to have a car?* In these cases the past tense is shown with the auxiliary verb *did* and *didn't*.

GRAMMAR – STUDY SHEET 4

Transitive and Intransitive Verbs

A <u>**transitive verb**</u> **requires an object** in the form of a noun or pronoun to complete its meaning. This **object answers the questions *who(m)* or *what*.**

Examples: -The students <u>**write**</u> **essays**.

   What do the students <u>**write**</u>? **Essays**.

   -Alan <u>**loves**</u> **Jane**.

   Who (m) does Alan <u>**love**</u>? **Jane**.

An <u>**intransitive verb**</u> is one that **does not require an object** to complete its meaning. The sentence may end with the verb, an adjective, or an adverb. The questions one may ask with these forms are ***when, where, how*, or *why*.**

Examples: - The children <u>sat</u>.

   - The children <u>sat</u> at 9:30 am. *(when or what time?)*

   - The children <u>sat</u> at their tables. *(where?)*
   - The children <u>sat</u> quietly.   *(how?)*
   - The children <u>sat</u> because their teacher told them to. *(why?)*

GRAMMAR – STUDY SHEET 5

Conditionals

Listed below are examples, uses and formation of conditionals followed by some exercises.

Examples	Use
1st Conditional • If it rains, I will stay at home. • Dave will buy a new car if he gets a promotion.	Often called the "real" conditional because it is used for real - or possible - situations. The first conditional is used to talk about the future or facts / situations which are true in the present and future.
2nd Conditional • If she studied more, she would pass her exams. • I would lower taxes if I were the Prime Minister. • They would buy a new house if they won the lottery.	Often called the "unreal" conditional because it is used for unreal - impossible or improbable (hypothetical) – situations. It is also used to give advice and express hopes and ambitions. This conditional offers an imaginary result for a given situation.
3rd Conditional • If he had seen Alan, he would have spoken to him. • Magda wouldn't have found a new job if she had stayed in Warsaw.	Often referred to as the "past" conditional because it concerns only past situations with hypothetical results. Used to express a hypothetical result to a past given situation (contrary to what really happened).

For information only:

Zero Conditional • If the temperature goes below freezing, water freezes. • She doesn't worry if Jack stays late after school.	Situations that are always true or factual.

GRAMMAR – STUDY SHEET 6

Articles *a, an* and *the*

A/an is used to say what **kind of thing someone or something is**.

Find an ashtray. She was an athlete. They're farmers.

A/an can denote **an example** of something. Plurals – no article.

A fly has wings. I'd like an orange juice. Bananas are yellow.

A/an can mean **a particular one**.

John married a nurse. They employed workmen.

There are many uses of the article *the*. Please refer to Swan, page 654.

GRAMMAR – STUDY SHEET 7

Reported Speech

Reported Statements
When do we use reported speech? Sometimes someone says a sentence, for example "I'm going to the theatre tonight". Later, maybe we want to tell someone else what the first person said.

We use a reporting verb like 'say' or 'tell'. If this verb is in the present tense, we just put 'she says' and then the sentence:

Direct speech: I like coffee.
Reported speech: She says she likes coffee.

We don't need to change the tense, though probably we do need to change the 'person' from 'I' to 'she', for example. We also may need to change words like 'my' and 'your'.

On the other hand, if the reporting verb is in the past tense, then usually we change the tenses in reported speech:

Direct speech: I like coffee.
Reported speech: She said she liked coffee.

Tense: Direct Speech/Reported Speech
Present simple I like coffee"
She said (that) she liked coffee.

Present continuous
I am living in Brighton"
She said she was living in Brighton.

Past simple "I bought a car."
 She said she had bought a bag OR She said she bought a bag.

2
Past continuous
"I was walking along the road."
She said she had been walking along the road.

Present perfect
"I haven't seen Jane." She said she hadn't seen Jane.

Past perfect* "I had taken driving lessons before."
She said she had taken driving lessons before.

Will "I'll see you tomorrow." She said she would see me tomorrow.

Would* "I would help, but I can't speak perfect English."
She said she would help but she couldn't speak perfect English."

Could* "I could swim when I was five." She said she could swim when she was five.

Shall "I shall visit later." She said she would visit later.

Should* "I should call my son." She said she should call her son.

Might* "I might be early." She said she might be early.

Must "I must study at the weekend."
She said she must study at the weekend OR She said she had to study at the weekend.

*Modal verbs are used we believe something is certain, probable or possible.

Printed in Great Britain
by Amazon